Mindfulness & Calm

Adventures in Ink
& Inspiration

This is a FLAME TREE book | First published 2016

Publisher and Creative Director: Nick Wells
Senior Project Editor: Laura Bulbeck
Digital Manager: Chris Herbert
Art Director: Mike Spender

Special thanks to Frances Bodiam

Images in this book were crafted at the Flame Tree Studio, based on illustrations
© copyright Curly Pat, Tania Anisimova, anfisa focusova, Ryani Kristina, ilonitta,
Jake Jackson, Nairina, Plotnikova Olga, Rodina Olena, Photo-Nuke, Saharinka,
Tashsat, tets, Yoko Design.

© Flame Tree Publishing Ltd 2016

FLAME TREE PUBLISHING
6 Melbray Mews, Fulham,
London SW6 3NS, United Kingdom

www.flametreepublishing.com

ISBN 978-1-78361-912-2

1 3 5 7 9 10 8 6 4 2
16 18 20 19 17

Printed in China | Created and designed in the UK

Mindfulness & Calm

Adventures in Ink & Inspiration

Words & Selection by Daisy Seal
Created by the Flame Tree Studio

FLAME TREE
PUBLISHING

My head, hot and fevered, rests upon the hills of my mind as I try to rest, and allow my thoughts to drift

From the buzz and drain of life. Patterns of the universe draw me upwards and I watch myself lift

Into the skies, watching my tense limbs from above, while I swim with clouds and play with butterflies,

Swirling in a circle around the world, teasing the dragons with laughter, and waiting for the moon to rise.

Mindfulness & Calm
Adventures in Ink & Inspiration

Such busy lives we lead! Sometimes we just need some relaxation and a little calm. This beautiful new book, created with a range of challenges, from easy and intermediate to the more detailed, will give you hours of calming entertainment. And now we've added a series of inspirational, mindful messages that weave through gently swirling backgrounds.

Mindfulness & Calm leads you through a series of reflections on life, our place in the universe, and our relationships with friends and family. The curl of vines, the flowing petals, and the symmetry of mandala patterns will provide that much needed rest from the chores and stresses of the day, helping us into a restful night's sleep.

As with the previous books Secret Places, Woodland Places and the companion to this title, Love & Friendship, you can use a variety of pens: from gel and pencil, to pigment and crayon, from ballpoint and rollerball to highlighters, although it's best to avoid the heavy felt pens.

We designed the book so you can either colour the page with the hidden messages, or the image on the back, which is the same, but without the words. Each page is perforated near the spine of the book, so you can tear out and frame, perhaps even send them as a gift to a loved one.

Don't forget to sign your name at the bottom of the page, when you've finished each picture...

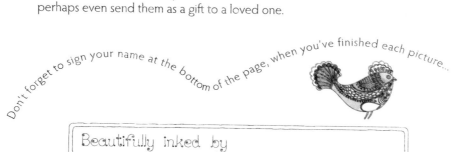

Beautifully inked by

Beautifully inked by

THERE IS NO NEED TO SUFFER IN SILENCE WHEN THE WORLD IS FULL OF EARS

Beautifully inked by

Beautifully inked by

HOPE, LIKE THE TWILIGHT SUN ALWAYS PROMISES TO RETURN

Beautifully inked by

Beautifully inked by

WHEN THE SUN BREAKS THROUGH THE STORM, IT BREACHES THE TROUBLED MIND

Beautifully inked by

Beautifully inked by

LET THE WARMTH OF HOPE FALL GENTLY ON YOUR TROUBLED MIND

Beautifully inked by

Beautifully inked by

Beautifully inked by

Beautifully inked by

Beautifully inked by

IN TIME, YOU WILL BALANCE THE FRENZY OF YOUR LIFE

Beautifully inked by

Beautifully inked by

FEEL THE FRAGRANT BREEZE OF TWILIGHT LIFT YOU INTO QUIET SLUMBER.

Beautifully inked by

Beautifully inked by

ONCE YOU'VE FOUND YOUR WAY TO INNER CALM, NURTURE IT QUIETLY.

Beautifully inked by

Beautifully inked by

Beautifully inked by

Beautifully inked by

AS THE SUN RISES IT LIFTS AWAY THE UNCERTAINTIES OF NIGHT.

Beautifully inked by

Beautifully inked by

TAKE COMFORT FROM THE PASSAGE OF THE SEASONS.

Beautifully inked by

Beautifully inked by

LET YOUR MIND SWIM WITH THE REFLECTIONS.

Beautifully inked by

Beautifully inked by

YOUR LIFE IS AN EVER-EXPANDING UNIVERSE. NEW EXPERIENCES EMERGE IN EVERY MOMENT.

Beautifully inked by

Beautifully inked by

MEDITATE AT SUNSET, AND FEEL THE WARMTH DRIFT FROM YOUR FACE INTO THE HORIZON.

Beautifully inked by

Beautifully inked by

SWIM GENTLY THROUGH THE CALM POOLS OF MEMORY.

Beautifully inked by

Beautifully inked by

FEEL THE SOFT FLUCTUATIONS OF NATURE ALL AROUND YOU.

Beautifully inked by

Beautifully inked by

YOU WILL FIND COMFORT IN THE STILLNESS DEEP WITHIN YOU.

Beautifully inked by

Beautifully inked by

THE CHILD WITHIN YOU REMAINS, STILL, ALTHOUGH SHE SLEEPS INSIDE.

Beautifully inked by

Beautifully inked by

RAIN GLISTENS ON YOUR FOREHEAD TURNING SUPRISE INTO QUIET JOY.

Beautifully inked by

Beautifully inked by

IN THE CROWDED OCEANS OF LIFE THERE ARE ISLANDS OF QUIET BEAUTY.

Beautifully inked by

Beautifully inked by

CALM YOUR BREATHING WITH THOUGHTS OF SUMMER BREEZES

Beautifully inked by

Beautifully inked by

UNDERNEATH THE FRAUGHT SURFACE OF THE NOW, THERE IS A QUIET SHIVER OF THE FUTURE.

Beautifully inked by

Beautifully inked by

AWAY FROM THE NOISE OF TECHNOLOGY, OPEN YOURSELF TO THE LANGUAGE OF STILLNESS.

Beautifully inked by

Beautifully inked by

THE SEARCH FOR INNER BALANCE ONLY REQUIRES INNER BEAUTY.

Beautifully inked by

Beautifully inked by

THERE ARE MANY STEPS TO RECOVERY, BUT TAKEN ONE AT A TIME, YOU'LL HARDLY NOTICE THE JOURNEY.

Beautifully inked by

Beautifully inked by

NEVER LOOK BACK TO SOMETHING YOU CANNOT CHANGE. KEEP YOUR EYES FORWARD.

Beautifully inked by

Beautifully inked by

Beautifully inked by

EVEN THE TREES GAZE IN AWE AT THE MOUNTAINS.

Beautifully inked by

Beautifully inked by

THE SUN WILL SHINE AGAIN. PART OF YOU WILL ALWAYS BE READY.

Beautifully inked by

Beautifully inked by

Beautifully inked by

TAKE SLOW DEEP BREATHS BEFORE YOU START YOUR DAY

Beautifully inked by

Beautifully inked by

THE SETTING SUN LEAVES A GENTLE PATH FOR YOU TO FOLLOW.

Beautifully inked by

Beautifully inked by

Beautifully inked by

IT TAKES A STEADY HAND TO DRAW THE DARKNESS FROM THE NIGHT.

Beautifully inked by

Beautifully inked by

TAKE SLOW, DEEP BREATHS BEFORE YOU START YOUR DAY.

Beautifully inked by

Beautifully inked by

THE SETTING
SUN LEAVES
A GENTLE
PATH FOR YOU
TO FOLLOW.

Beautifully inked by

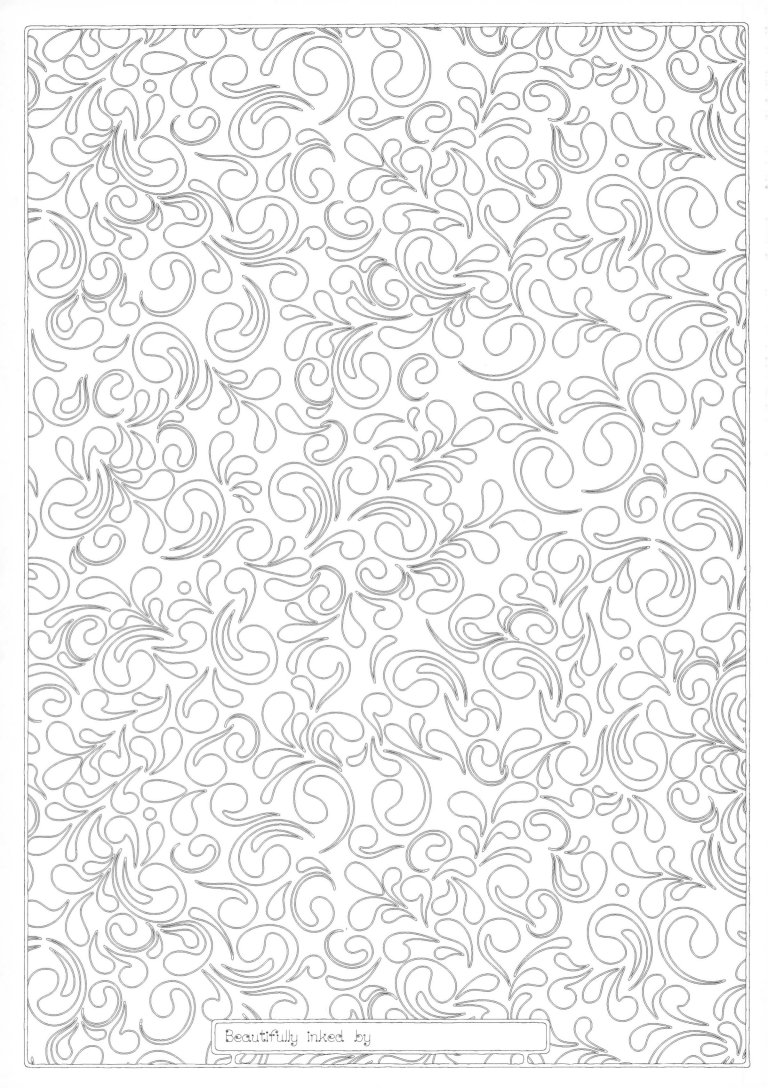

Beautifully inked by

Beautifully inked by

Beautifully inked by

Beautifully inked by

Beautifully inked by

ALWAYS REMEMBER THE KINDNESS AND GENEROSITY OF OTHERS.

Beautifully inked by

Beautifully inked by

EVEN THE MOST NEGLECTED CORNERS OF YOUR LIFE CAN REVEAL A HIDDEN BEAUTY.

Beautifully inked by

Beautifully inked by

YOU ARE NOT WRONG TO BE DIFFERENT. YOU ARE NOT DIFFERENT IF YOU ARE WRONG.

Beautifully inked by

Beautifully inked by

THE SEA OFFERS A GLIMPSE AT THE VASTNESS OF THE UNIVERSE.

Beautifully inked by

Beautifully inked by

BREAK WITH THE PAST AND EMERGE FROM THE HEAVY HAND OF SADNESS.

Beautifully inked by

Beautifully inked by

PETALS ON THE WATER FALL WITHOUT CARE, OFFERING THEMSELVES UP TO THE CURRENTS.

Beautifully inked by

Beautifully inked by

ON WAKING,
THE LIGHT INTRUDES
ON THE DARKNESS
AND SETS FLIGHT
TO ITS MISERIES.

Beautifully inked by

Beautifully inked by

JUST TO STAND AND BREATHE THE STILL, COOL AIR CAN BE THE GREATEST TREASURE OF ALL.

Beautifully inked by

Beautifully inked by

WE SHARE DETERMINATION IN OUR STRENGTH, TOGETHER.

Beautifully inked by

Beautifully inked by

IMAGINE SILVER SPIRITS BENEATH THE SURFACE OF THE WATER, RISING AND FALLING WITH YOUR MOOD

Beautifully inked by

Beautifully inked by

Beautifully inked by

SMALL STEPS, EVERY DAY OFFER, THE PROMISE OF REVIVAL

Beautifully inked by

Beautifully inked by

LITTLE POCKETS OF CALM CAN OVERCOME A LANDSCAPE OF ANXIETY.

Beautifully inked by

Beautifully inked by

Beautifully inked by

LOOK BEYOND THE IMMEDIATE AND BE ENSPIRED BY DISTANT HILLS

Beautifully inked by

Beautifully inked by

TAKE TIME TO REVEL IN THE SIMPLE JOY OF NATURAL SPACES.

Beautifully inked by

Beautifully inked by

FOCUS ON A DISTANT POINT AND ALLOW ALL THOUGHTS TO FALL AWAY.

Beautifully inked by

Beautifully inked by

IN YOUR SLEEP YOUR MIND WILL DANCE LIKE AN ANCIENT SPIRIT

Beautifully inked by

Beautifully inked by

MEMORIES, LIKE FOOTPRINTS IN THE SNOW, TRAIL ACROSS YOUR MIND, SEEKING ANSWERS.

Beautifully inked by

Visual Arts

FLAME TREE PUBLISHING
flametreepublishing.com

From **How to Draw Manga** to **Tattoo Art**,
Alphonse Mucha to **Drawing Basics**, we publish
a range of fine and practical books, calendars and
journals for artists and art enthusiasts.

If you enjoyed this book, please sign up for updates,
information and offers on further titles on the visual arts at
blog.flametreepublishing.com/art-of-fine-gifts/